GUINEA PIG PALS

Crabtree Publishing Company
www.crabtreebooks.com
1-800-387-7650

Published in Canada
Crabtree Publishing
616 Welland Avenue
St. Catharines, ON
L2M 5V6

Published in the United States
Crabtree Publishing
PMB 59051
350 Fifth Ave, 59th Floor
New York, NY 10118

Published in 2018 by CRABTREE PUBLISHING COMPANY.

First published in 2017 by Wayland
Copyright © Hodder and Stoughton, 2017

Author: Pat Jacobs

Editor: Elizabeth Brent

Project coordinator: Kathy Middleton

Editor: Petrice Custance

Cover and Interior Design: Dynamo

Proofreader: Wendy Scavuzzo

Prepress technician: Samara Parent

Print and production coordinator: Margaret Amy Salter

Photographs:
iStock: p1 ksena32; p2 LuminaStock, mwpenny, Mingzhe Zhang; p4 adogslifephoto; p6 photokdk, svehlik, cynoclub, Gemma Rose Amos; p7 krithnarong, Farinosa, GlobalP; p8 adogslifephoto, Farinosa, Olesya Tseytlin, cynoclub, GlobalP; p9 DevMarya, terry6970, leaf; p11 RomeoLu, Dantyya; p12 DevMarya, JohnatAPW; p13 Ocskaymark, Eric Isselée; p14 icarmen13, Andrzej Tokarski, 13-Smile; p15 Elena Blokhina, eve_eve01genesis, Mr_Mozymov; p16 Mendelex_photography; p17 eAlisa, scigelova; p19 Crisalexo, Marco Hegner, Eric Isselée; p20 Azaliya; p21 n1kcy, Ralph Loesche, kosobu; p23 VikaRayu, p24 AnastasiaGlazneva, Lari Huttunen; p26 ksena32; p27 Zsolt Farkas, daizuoxin, ALLEKO, Cloud7Days, cynoclub; p28 Eric Isselée, Ramona smiers; p3, 29 Arkhipov; p32 GlobalP; Front cover: photokdk; Back cover: Vassiliy Vishnevskiy

Shutterstock: p7 joannawnuk; p10 marilyn barbone; p16 Dora Zett; p18 melis; p26 ADA_photo

Alamy: p5 Juniors Bildarchiv GmbH; p17 petographer; p19 Maximilian Weinzierl; p20 Juniors Bildarchiv GmbH; p22 imageBROKER; p23 Petra Wegner; p25 Maximilian Weinzierl, Juniors Bildarchiv GmbH; p26 Juniors Bildarchiv GmbH; p27 petographer, imageBROKER

Printed in the USA/072017/CG20170524

Library and Archives Canada Cataloguing in Publication

Jacobs, Pat, author
    Guinea pig pals / Pat Jacobs.

(Pet pals)
Includes index.
Issued in print and electronic formats.
ISBN 978-0-7787-3552-6 (hardcover).--
ISBN 978-0-7787-3581-6 (softcover).--
ISBN 978-1-4271-1946-9 (HTML)

        1. Guinea pigs as pets--Juvenile literature. 2. Guinea pigs--Behavior--Juvenile literature. I. Title.

SF459.G9J33 2017   j636.935'92   C2017-902517-1
                                                                      C2017-902518-X

Library of Congress Cataloging-in-Publication Data

Names: Jacobs, Pat, author.
Title: Guinea pig pals / Pat Jacobs.
Description: New York, New York : Crabtree Publishing, 2018. |
    Series: Pet pals | Audience: Age 7-10. | Audience: Grade K to 3. |
    Includes index.
Identifiers: LCCN 2017016737 (print) | LCCN 2017027434 (ebook) |
    ISBN 9781427119469 (Electronic HTML) |
    ISBN 9780778735526 (reinforced library binding) |
    ISBN 9780778735816 (pbk.)
Subjects: LCSH: Guinea pigs as pets--Juvenile literature.
Classification: LCC SF459.G9 (ebook) | LCC SF459.G9 J33 2018 (print)
    | DDC 636.935/92--dc23
LC record available at https://lccn.loc.gov/2017016737

CONTENTS

YOUR GUINEA PIG
FROM HEAD TO TAIL

Spanish sailors brought guinea pigs to Europe from South America in the 16th century. At the time, they were so expensive only wealthy people could afford them. Thanks to their gentle, friendly nature, guinea pigs have become popular pets around the world.

Ears: Excellent hearing helps guinea pigs to identify **predators** before they come into view.

Legs: Guinea pig legs aren't very strong, and they break easily, so don't let your pet fall or jump from any height.

Feet: Sharp claws help wild guinea pigs to climb mountainsides and walk on difficult ground.

Eyes: Guinea pigs' large eyes are high on the sides of their head, so they can see predators coming from all directions, but they can't see right in front of their nose!

Brain: Guinea pigs have a very good memory for pathways leading to food sources.

Whiskers: Sensitive whiskers help guinea pigs to find their way in the dark, and to detect food and other objects in the blind spot in front of their nose.

Teeth: Like all **rodents**, a guinea pig's front teeth will continually grow. They spend most of their time chewing, though, which wears the teeth down.

Nose: Guinea pigs have a good sense of smell, and recognize their companions and owners by their scent.

GUINEA PIG FACTS

- Guinea pigs usually live for five to eight years, but a British guinea pig named Snowball died at the age of 14 years and 10 months.

- The proper name for a guinea pig is a cavy. No one knows how they got their common name because they don't come from Guinea, Africa, and they are not related to pigs!

GUINEA PIG BREEDS

Guinea pigs are all a similar size and, although they have individual personalities, their **temperament** is more or less the same whatever their **breed**.

Abyssinian guinea pigs are easy to spot. They have a unique coat because their hair grows in swirls, which are sometimes called rosettes.

American guinea pigs have short, smooth hair and come in many different color combinations. Their short coats make them easy to look after.

Peruvians are one of the oldest breeds of guinea pigs. They have very long hair, which grows over their face, and they need regular grooming, bathing, and trimming.

Rex guinea pigs have thick hair that stands on end, drooping ears, and curly whiskers. They are easy to care for and make very good pets.

Shelties (or Silkies) have long, soft hair that is swept back, so it doesn't grow over the guinea pig's face. They have to be brushed and trimmed regularly.

Teddy guinea pigs have thick, wiry hair all over their bodies, which makes them look cuddly and round. They need brushing once a week.

Skinny pigs are almost hairless, which means they need a warm place to live and a high-energy diet. Their skin is very sensitive, so they need soft bedding, sunscreen when outside, and regular moisturizing.

Texels are high-maintenance pets. Their long, curly coats need a lot of attention to stop them from tangling and getting dirty.

CHOOSING YOUR GUINEA PIG

In the wild, guinea pigs live in small groups, made up of a male, several females, and their pups. They get lonely on their own, so pet guinea pigs should be kept in pairs or groups.

MALE **OR** FEMALE?

You should get a single-sex pair or group. Females usually live happily together, but unless males know each other well, they may fight at first while they sort out who's in charge.

LONG- **OR** SHORT-HAIRED?

Short-haired guinea pigs are easy to look after, but those with longer hair need daily grooming, along with regular trimming and bathing. Guinea pigs don't always enjoy this but it is essential for their well-being.

INDOOR **OR** OUTDOOR PET?

Guinea pigs can live indoors, but they need a quiet space because they have sensitive hearing. Outdoor piggies should have a cage in a sheltered place, with a cozy sleeping area. If it gets really cold, you may need to bring them inside.

PET CHECK ☑

Before you buy or adopt a guinea pig, make sure that:

- its teeth meet properly
- its eyes are sparkling
- its coat is shiny
- it doesn't have sores on its feet or legs
- it walks normally

BUY **OR** ADOPT?

If you want a particular type of guinea pig, you may have to buy it from a **breeder**. But there are many guineas in rescue centers that are looking for new homes. Your local animal shelter might have the perfect pair for you.

HOME COMFORTS

Guinea pig hutches should be large enough to give each animal at least 10 square feet (1 square meter) of space, and they must be completely predator-proof. Animals that attack guinea pigs include foxes, rats, dogs, cats, and birds of prey.

DOS AND DON'TS

- **Do** keep the cage in a sheltered spot, where guinea pigs won't get too hot or too cold.

- **Do** cover the base with newspaper to make it easy to clean.

- **Do** give your guinea pigs a chance to run around every day, either indoors or in an outside enclosure.

- **Don't** keep guinea pigs in a garage with a car because the fumes could kill them.

- **Don't** use straw as bedding because it can poke your piggies in the eye.

- **Don't** put an outside run on grass that has been treated with weed killer.

Hay makes the best bedding—and guinea pigs can nibble on it if they feel like a midnight snack.

The hutch should be raised off the ground.

PET TALK

I can't sweat when I get hot, so please keep me in the shade.

There should be a dark area for sleeping and a light area with a wire-mesh door so your pets have fresh air.

Hutches should have solid floors because wire floors can damage guinea pigs' feet and legs.

OUT TO GRASS

Guinea pigs love to nibble fresh grass, so if you have a lawn, they will enjoy being outside in a run during the day. They'll need water and a hiding place in case they get scared.

INDOOR PLAY

An indoor run is perfect for guinea pigs in colder weather. The walls don't have to be very high because they're not great climbers. They are easily disturbed by loud noises, so they'll need a little hiding spot in case they feel nervous.

GET TO KNOW YOUR GUINEAS

Have the hutch, food, and water ready and waiting for your guinea pigs when you bring them home. They will probably be very nervous after their journey and will run for cover as soon as you put them inside the hutch.

PET TALK

I'm very timid, so it might take me a while to get used to being picked up.

SETTLING IN

Give your new pets a week to settle in before you start to handle them. Let them get to know you during this time by feeding them some tasty treats through the wires of their cage.

MAKING FRIENDS

When you're ready to hold your guinea pig, sit down on the floor and ask an adult to put the guinea pig on your lap. Stroke it gently while you offer it a vegetable treat.

OTHER PETS

However friendly your cat or dog might be, its scent will make guinea pigs nervous, so they should be kept apart. Rabbits often bully or kick guinea pigs, and may carry a disease that can harm piggies, so they don't make good cagemates.

If one of a guinea pig pair dies, you may want to get a new buddy for your remaining pet. If so, you will need to introduce them slowly.

INTRODUCING TWO GUINEA PIGS

A guinea pig may attack a new guinea pig that is suddenly put in its cage. Instead, place both guinea pigs in a new enclosure that doesn't smell like either of them, with some food to distract them. Watch the piggies carefully. They may chase each other at first, but they should soon become friends.

GUINEA PIG GRUB

A guinea pig's main food should be good-quality hay. It is similar to their diet in the wild, and chewing hay helps to stop a guinea pig's teeth from growing too long. Any leftover hay makes a soft covering for the cage floor.

PET TALK

Please don't feed me avocado, beans, rhubarb, onions, garlic, buttercups, or too much lettuce.

Guinea pigs find their food by smell, so watch out. If your fingers smell like carrots, your piggy may take a bite!

Guinea pigs love:

- Fresh grass
- Dandelions
- Clover
- Fresh herbs
- Cucumber
- Carrot (not too much)
- Melon
- Apple (no seeds)
- Banana
- Strawberries

DOUBLE DIGESTION

Guinea pigs make the most of their food by eating it twice. As well as hard droppings, guinea pigs also produce soft droppings which they eat. The soft droppings are full of protein and vitamins and are very important for a guinea pig's health.

FIVE-A-DAY

Guinea pigs, like humans, are among the few animals that don't make Vitamin C in their bodies. This means that, just like us, they need to eat fresh vegetables and fruit to stay healthy. Each guinea pig should have about a cupful every day.

Nuggets and pellets made especially for guinea pigs contain all the **nutrition** your piggies need. Be sure not to give them nuggets and pellets for rabbits though, because they don't contain Vitamin C.

NUGGETS AND PELLETS

If given mixed food, such as fruit and pellets, guinea pigs will pick out their favorite bits first, such as the fruit, and leave the pellets behind. The pellets are important for their health though, so be sure not to refill the bowl until all the food is gone.

DAY-TO-DAY CARE

Guinea pigs are easy to look after compared to many other pets, but they still need daily care. Learn to recognize their normal behavior, so you can quickly notice if something is wrong.

PICKING UP YOUR PIGGY

A wiggly guinea pig is hard to hold and may be injured if it falls, so ask an adult to carry your pet until it knows you well enough to relax. Pick it up by sliding one hand under its stomach and cup its bottom with your other hand. Hold it firmly (not tightly) against your chest, so it feels safe.

CLAW CLIPPING

Pet guinea pigs don't walk on rough ground like their wild relatives do, so their claws often grow too long. If you notice that your piggy's claws need clipping, ask an adult to do it while you distract your pet with a treat.

BATHING

Short-haired guinea pigs rarely need bathing unless they get especially dirty, but long-haired pets should be bathed about once a month. Use special guinea pig shampoo and make sure your pets are completely dry before they go outside.

GROOMING

Brush or comb your guinea pig gently from head to tail. This will help your pet to get used to being handled, and it gives you a chance to check that it doesn't have any injuries. Long-haired piggies should be groomed every day.

Let your pets run free on an easy-to-clean floor. Tell your family to watch out for the piggies and keep other pets out of the room.

PET TALK

My wild relatives are very active. I'm just like them, and need lots of exercise too!

HEALTH AND SAFETY

Guinea pigs hide injuries or illness because predators target weak animals, so it's important for owners to watch for any changes in their behavior. For example, if a guinea pig refuses treats, something is likely wrong.

MITES

If your guinea pig is scratching its skin, losing hair, and suddenly doesn't like being touched, it may have **mites.** These tiny creatures dig into a guinea pig's skin and cause terrible itching. This is a very painful condition that could kill your pet, so it needs to be treated right away.

Guinea pigs should be checked regularly for ear mites, especially if they are scratching their ears.

NEUTER/SPAY

Guinea pigs are not usually **neutered** or **spayed** because it is a big operation for such a small animal. As well, neutering does not stop male guinea pigs from fighting. Instead, guinea pigs are kept in pairs or groups of the same sex so that no baby guinea pigs are born.

BUMBLEFOOT

Bumblefoot is a painful **infection** of a guinea pig's foot. It happens when **bacteria** get into sores caused by wire cage floors or rough bedding. Check for swelling on the bottom of your pet's feet during grooming sessions.

Wire floors can injure guinea pigs' feet and increase the risk of bumblefoot.

PET TALK

I love to chew, so please make sure all electrical cables are out of my reach. I could get very badly hurt!

OUTDOOR DANGERS

Predators pose the biggest risk to outdoor guinea pigs. Foxes are very determined and can tip over lighter cages, slide open latches, and chew their way into hutches. They will also dig under runs, so never leave your pets in their run overnight.

GUINEA PIG BEHAVIOR

SCENT-MARKING

Guinea pigs are **territorial** animals and they **scent-mark** their home by rubbing their chin, cheeks, and bottom on everything in their cage. They may also do this in areas where they are allowed to run free.

Guinea pigs are creatures of habit. They don't like change, and they are happiest when their owners stick to the same daily schedule of feeding, cleaning, exercise, and cuddling.

TAKING COVER

In the wild, guinea pigs are food for many predators, including birds, so they are naturally nervous in open spaces. Your pet piggies may feel uncomfortable without a roof over their heads, so they should always have a place to hide, even indoors.

POPCORNING

When piggies are happy, they sometimes run back and forth and jump into the air while kicking their legs out. This joyful behavior is nicknamed "popcorning" because it resembles popcorn kernels popping! It is more common to see younger guinea pigs popcorning, but happy adults can as well.

FREEZING

When guinea pigs are startled by a strange sound, or sense danger, they often freeze to make themselves invisible to predators. They may also make a short vibrating noise to warn the rest of the group.

SLEEPING

Guinea pigs don't sleep for long periods. Instead, they take short naps throughout the day and night. Guinea pigs have an extra, **transparent** eyelid that allows them to sleep with their eyes open. This means they can be on the alert for predators.

PET TALK

Please feed me at the same time every day. I may not have a watch, but I know when it's dinner time!

COMMUNICATION

Guinea pigs are chatty little creatures. They talk to each other all the time, and they'll talk to you, too, especially if they think they might get a treat!

WHEEKING

Guinea pig owners will quickly learn to recognize this special sound that guinea pigs make when they're begging for food. Opening the fridge, cutting up vegetables, or rustling bags will be enough to get your piggies wheeking.

TEETH CHATTERING

When guinea pigs are about to fight, the hairs on their back stand on end, they yawn widely, and their teeth chatter. This may happen if you introduce two males that don't know each other. The best way to avoid a battle is to put a towel over one of them and take him away.

PET TALK

If I yawn, it's not because I'm tired. I'm opening my mouth to show off my sharp teeth.

PURRING AND RUMBLING

Purring and rumbling are vibrating sounds that have different meanings. A guinea pig may purr when it's being stroked, or to reassure itself in a new situation. Rumbling is a deeper sound and normally means the guinea pig is unhappy or scared.

BOSSY BEHAVIOR

When guinea pigs meet, they need to decide who's the boss. "Rumblestrutting" is part of this behavior. They make a rumbling sound and wiggle their hips slowly from side to side. This is often followed by the piggies running in a circle, nose to tail, and jumping on each other's backs.

23

TRAINING

Guinea pigs love eating and they can be trained to obey simple commands in return for a treat. Some will even learn to use a litter box. Never punish your pet if it doesn't do as you ask, because it will learn to be afraid of you.

SIT UP AND BEG

Sitting up is natural behavior for guinea pigs, so it's quite easy to teach your pet to sit by holding a treat above its head and saying the word "Sit!" Once your piggy has learned the command, it will sit when you tell it to and wait for its treat.

COME, PIGGY!

You can teach your guinea pig to come when you call by saying its name each time you give it a treat. Once your pet has learned that it will get a reward when it hears its name, try calling it during indoor exercise time.

LITTER TRAINING

Place a litter tray in the corner of the cage where you find the most droppings. Put some hay in the tray and scatter a few droppings on top. Your guinea pigs may not use their tray all the time, but if most of the droppings are in the same place, cleaning the cage will be easier.

Cat litter isn't suitable for guinea pigs because it's dusty and may cause breathing problems.

JUMPING THROUGH HOOPS

Stand a hoop on the ground in front of your guinea pig and hold a treat on the other side. When your piggy steps through the hoop, give it the treat and repeat this until it has mastered the trick. Now raise the hoop slightly off the ground so your piggy has to jump through it.

FUN AND GAMES

Guinea pigs love to run around, so they'll need some exercise time in their run, or in a safe space indoors, every day. You'll have fun watching them as they chase each other and explore.

GUINEA PIG ACTIVITY CENTER

Make an indoor play area and outside run more fun for your piggies by adding chew toys and balls. You can also make hiding spots with paper bags or newspaper, and add tunnels made of wide plastic or cardboard tubes.

Climbing is good exercise for guinea pigs, but make sure they won't injure themselves if they fall.

MAKE A MAZE

Create a maze using cardboard boxes joined together with tube tunnels. You can make the maze longer by adding more boxes and tubes. Place a guinea pig at each end of the maze, and see if they can find each other.

PET TALK

I'm most active in the early mornings and early evenings, so that's the best time to let me out for a run.

FIND THE FOOD

Hide your guinea pigs' favorite treats inside a cardboard tube stuffed with hay or balls of paper, and watch your piggies try to get them.

GUINEA PIG QUIZ

How much do you know about your guinea pig pal? Try this quiz to find out.

1 Which part of the world do guinea pigs come from?

a. Australia
b. South America
c. Spain

2 Which of these is another name for a guinea pig?

a. Cavy
b. Capybara
c. Coati

3 Why shouldn't you use straw as bedding?

a. It's very expensive
b. It's poisonous for guinea pigs
c. It may poke guinea pigs in the eye

4 Which of these guinea pig breeds has long, curly hair?

a. Teddy
b. Abyssinian
c. Texel

5 What is bumblefoot?

a. A dance guinea pigs perform when they first meet
b. A painful foot infection
c. A breed of guinea pig

6 **Why don't rabbits make good cage mates for guinea pigs?**

a. They can pass on a disease to guinea pigs
b. They may kick and bully them
c. Both of these

10 **How often should you groom a long-haired guinea pig?**

a. Every day
b. Every week
c. Every month

7 **Which of these foods is bad for guinea pigs?**

a. Cucumber
b. Avocado
c. Apple

8 **What is "popcorning"?**

a. Hiding from predators
b. Calling for food
c. Jumping in the air

9 **When are guinea pigs most active?**

a. At night
b. Early morning and early evening
c. At lunchtime

QUIZ ANSWERS

1 Which part of the world do guinea pigs come from?

b. South America

2 Which of these is another name for a guinea pig?

a. Cavy

3 Why shouldn't you use straw as bedding?

c. It may poke guinea pigs in the eye

4 Which of these guinea pig breeds has long, curly hair?

c. Texel

5 What is bumblefoot?

b. A painful foot infection

6 Why don't rabbits make good cage mates for guinea pigs?

c. Both of these

7 Which of these foods is bad for guinea pigs?

b. Avocado

8 What is "popcorning"?

c. Jumping in the air

9 When are guinea pigs most active?

b. Early morning and early evening

10 How often should you groom a long-haired guinea pig?

a. Every day

LEARNING MORE

BOOKS

Howell, Laura. *Looking After Guinea Pigs*. Harper Collins, 2013.

Kalman, Bobbie, and Kelley MacAulay. *Guinea Pigs*. Crabtree Publishing, 2004.

Vanderlip, Sharon. *The Guinea Pig Handbook*. Barron's Educational Series, 2015.

WEBSITES

www.lovethatpet.com/small-pets/guinea-pig/
This website is full of helpful information about guinea pig care.

http://pbskids.org/itsmylife/family/pets/article7.html
Check out this site for fun pet facts and great tips on caring for your guinea pig.

www.humanesociety.org/animals/guinea_pigs/tips/guinea_pig_tips.html
Visit this site for all kinds of tips on how to be the perfect pal to your guinea pig.

GLOSSARY

bacteria Microscopic living things, such as germs, that can cause disease

breed A group of animals with the same ancestors and characteristics

breeder A person who raises particular breeds of animals

infection When bacteria enters the body of a human or an animal and causes illness or disease

mite A tiny creature similar to a spider

neuter An operation that stops male animals from being able to make babies

nutrition The process of a human or an animal eating the foods they require to be healthy

predator An animal that hunts and eats other animals

rodent A type of animal whose teeth grow throughout their life

scent-mark When an animal releases an odor or substance, such as urine, to mark their territory

spay An operation that stops female animals from being able to have babies

temperament The way a human or an animal behaves

territorial When an animal claims an area for itself and defends it against intruders

transparent Clear or see-through

INDEX